W9-BMB-323

Reed New Zealand Nature Series

Common Birds

in New Zealand 1

Reed New Zealand Nature Series

Common Birds

in New Zealand 1

Town, Open Country and Wetland Birds

Geoff Moon

REED

Cover: Pukeko at nest with newly hatched chick.
Title page: Male New Zealand Kingfisher.

Established in 1907, Reed Publishing (NZ) Ltd
is New Zealand's largest book publisher, with over 300 titles in print.

For details on all these books visit our website:
www.reed.co.nz

Published by Reed Books, a division of Reed Publishing (NZ) Ltd,
39 Rawene Rd, Birkenhead, Auckland 10. Associated companies, branches and
representatives throughout the world.

ISBN 0 7900 0369 4
First published 1995
Reprinted 2000, 2002

Printed in New Zealand

Contents

Introduction

New Zealand is blessed with a wide variety of habitats where birds live, feed and breed. These localities include our towns and cities as well as mountains, forests, wetlands (fresh water habitats), open country and coasts.

Common Birds in New Zealand is the first of two volumes on the common or commonly seen birds of New Zealand. By this is meant that they are either prolific in numbers, distributed throughout many parts of the country, or that a visitor to the area in which they are most common will probably see them. In addition to native and endemic species, the numerous introduced birds which have become an integral part of the New Zealand bird fauna are included.

The book is not designed as a comprehensive field guide, but rather for use in practical visual identification. Colour photographs are complemented by a brief summary of information, designed more as an incentive for further interest and study than as an exhaustive reference. Scientific language has been kept to a minimum when giving descriptions and, where used, has been explained.

The species chosen for Volume 1 covering *Town, Open Country and Wetland* are not the only birds seen in these habitats, nor are these the only areas in which they are always found. Some birds, such as the Kingfisher or the Silvereye, can be seen in various habitats. However, some arbitrary decisions were required as to which volume certain species were to be placed in. Many of the introduced birds were confined to Volume 1. Volume 2 covering *Mountain,*

Forest and Shore habitats records predominantly native and endemic species prominent in those parts of the country least modified by humans. Volume 3 covers the *Rare* birds of New Zealand: those rarely seen, those very small in number, and those endangered.

In some bird species sexual dimorphism occurs, where there is a marked difference in the plumage colour between the sexes. In each instance where this is evident, photographs have been included to illustrate this feature.

Taxonomists group birds into specific sections according to their anatomy. Closely related species are listed as a genus, while related genera are grouped together as a family. These families in turn are grouped to form an order. The first part of a bird's scientific name is the genus. The second name refers to the species, and the third name, where applicable, refers to the subspecies. Thus, dealing with the Welcome Swallow, the order is Passeriformes (perching birds), the family is Hirundinidae (Swallows), the genus is *Hirundo,* the species is *tahitica* and the subspecies is *neoxena.*

In this volume, the family, genus, species and subspecies are described. Common names and Maori names (where applicable) are given. The orders and families by which the birds in this volume are categorised are listed after this Introduction.

Birds are dealt with in the same order (according to anatomy) as in the *Checklist of the Birds of New Zealand,* 3rd edition, compiled by the Checklist Committee (E.G. Turbott, Convener) of the Ornithological Society of New Zealand Inc., and published in 1990 by Random Century.

Species are divided into three categories:

- *Endemic* — originating in New Zealand and confined solely to the New Zealand region, e.g. Kiwi.
- *Native* — naturally occurring in New Zealand, but also found elsewhere in the world, e.g. Pukeko is also found in Australia and South Africa; often self-introduced from other countries.
- *Introduced* — introduced by human agency, e.g. Blackbird.

Nearly all native and endemic birds in New Zealand are protected. Most are fully protected, although some, such as the Pukeko, may be hunted in their particular open season.

The size of each bird is given in centimetres, and is its length from bill tip to tail tip and, in a few instances, the length of the legs extending beyond the tail. Note that the length measurement is only a general guide to the overall size of the bird; some birds are long and thin.

I would like to acknowledge the kind assistance of the many friends who have helped me with advice, or have provided opportunities to obtain photographs.

I hope that readers find this book useful and informative, and that it stimulates further interest.

Geoff Moon

Orders and Families Represented in this Volume

Order   Podicipediformes: Grebes
Family   Podicipedidae: Grebes

Order   Pelecaniformes: Gannets and Cormorants
Family   Phalacrocoracidae: Cormorants and Shags

Order   Ciconiiformes: Herons, Bitterns and Egrets
Family   Ardeidae: Herons and Bitterns

Order   Anseriformes: Duck-like birds
Family   Anatidae: Swans, Geese and Ducks

Order   Falconiformes: Diurnal birds of prey
Family   Accipitridae: Hawks
           Falconidae: Falcons

Order   Galliformes: Game birds
Family   Phasianidae: Partridges, Quails and Pheasants

Order   Gruiformes: Rails
Family   Rallidae: Rails and Coots

Order   Charadriiformes: Waders, Gulls and Terns
Family   Charadriidae: Dotterels and Plovers

Order   Columbiformes: Pigeons and Doves
Family   Columbidae: Pigeons and Doves

| Order | Psittaciformes: Cockatoos and Parrots |
| Family | Cacatuidae: Cockatoos |

| Order | Strigiformes: Owls |
| Family | Strigidae: Owls |

| Order | Coraciiformes: Kingfishers |
| Family | Alcedinidae: Kingfishers |

Order	Passeriformes: Perching birds
Family	Alaudidae: Larks
	Motacillidae: Pipits
	Hirundinidae: Swallows
	Muscicapidae: Warblers, Thrushes
	Prunellidae: Accentors (Sparrow-like song birds)
	Sylviidae: Old World Warblers (Fernbirds)
	Emberizidae: Buntings, Cardinals (Yellowhammer)
	Fringillidae: Finches
	Ploceidae: Weaver Birds (House Sparrow)
	Sturnidae: Starlings and Oxpeckers
	Cracticidae: Bell Magpies
	Corvidae: Crows and Jays

New Zealand Dabchick / Weweia
Poliocephalus rufopectus

Family PODICIPEDIDAE
Genus *Poliocephalus*

Category
- Endemic.

Field Characteristics
- 28 cm. Half size of Grey Duck.
- Recognised by small head, sharp bill. Blunt rear with no tail, rump high when swimming.
- Throat and upper chest reddish brown. Underparts white with brown mottling on flanks. Immature coloration: cheeks grey, throat and upper chest pale reddish brown, underparts white.
- Entirely aquatic. Dives for food, submerging for 10 to 25 seconds.
- Low, skimming flight during courtship. Thought to migrate to other lakes at night.

Voice
- Usually silent, but weak chattering call and moan near nest.

◀ **New Zealand Dabchick.**
◀ **New Zealand Dabchick with 2¹/₂-week-old chicks.**

Food
- Dives for small fish, crustaceans, insects and tadpoles.

Breeding
- *Time:* Long nesting season, usually July to March.
- *Nest:* Floating nest of water weeds anchored to raupo or rushes. Also builds nests of weeds on firm ground under rock overhangs or boatsheds.
- *Eggs:* Clutch of 2 or 3 white eggs which soon become stained after being covered with weed when unattended. Both sexes incubate for 21 to 24 days.
- *Chicks:* striped plumage; carried on backs of swimming parents.

Distribution & Habitat
- North Island lakes, ponds and dams. Commonest on coastal sand-dune lakes and lakes of central Volcanic Plateau.
- Post-nuptial flocks on lakes of Wairarapa and Manawatu.
- Now absent from South Island.

Black Shag (Black Cormorant)/Kawau

Phalacrocorax carbo novaehollandiae

Family PHALACROCORACIDAE
Genus *Phalacrocorax*

Category

- Native. A cosmopolitan species, it is also found in Australia, Europe, Africa, Asia and North America.

Field Characteristics

- 88 cm. New Zealand's largest shag.
- Black with a white thigh patch, and greenish black head plumes in the breeding season. Immature coloration is browner than the adult with lighter undersides.
- Flies with alternate wingbeat and glides.
- Often seen perched on a rock in lakes, or in flocks on sandspits and shellbanks in marine habitats.

◀ **Black Shags, male and female, at nest.**
▼ **Black Shag (Black Cormorant).**

Voice

- Raucous guttural calls at nesting sites, otherwise silent.

Food

- Feeds by diving from surface.
- Eats live fish, especially eels, and crustaceans. Fish are swallowed head first.

Breeding

- *Time:* During many months of the year, generally April to May and September to October.
- *Nest:* In colonies on ledges of cliffs or on the ground on small islands, also sometimes in trees.
- *Eggs:* Clutch of 3 or 4 chalky white eggs is incubated by both sexes for 28 to 30 days.
- *Chicks:* Fledge when 7 weeks old.

Distribution & Habitat

- Common on inland lakes and sheltered coasts.

3 Little Black Shag
Phalacrocorax sulcirostris

Family PHALACROCORACIDAE
Genus *Phalacrocorax*

Category
Native. Also found in Australia and Southwest Pacific.

Field Characteristics
- 61 cm. Slightly smaller than Little Shag.
- Its long narrow bill and glossy plumage distinguish it from the black-plumaged immature Little Shag.
- No crest.
- Often seen in groups.

Voice
- Croaking and clicking sounds when fishing.
- Whistles and croaks at nest.

◀ **A nesting colony of Little Black Shags.**

◀ **Little Black Shags (Little Black Cormorants).**

Food
- Small fish, crustaceans and insects.
- Feeds by diving from surface. Often several birds fish in a pack; birds in the rear leapfrog to front of pack.

Breeding
- *Time:* Peak laying periods in spring and autumn: September to December, February to May.
- *Nest:* In small colonies in trees or bushes near water, often in association with Little Shags. Nests are of sticks.
- *Eggs:* 3 or 4 pale blue eggs with chalky covering. Both sexes incubate; period uncertain.

Distribution & Habitat
- Uncommon in the South Island.
- Inhabits freshwater lakes and sheltered coastal waters.

▲ Little Shag, white-throated plumage phase.

Little Shag/Kawaupaka
Phalacrocorax melanoleucos brevirostris

Family PHALACROCORACIDAE
Genus *Phalacrocorax*

Category
• Native. Also found in Australia and Southwest Pacific.

Field Characteristics
• 56 cm. Slightly larger than Little Black Shag.
• Long tail.
• Mostly black with a short yellow bill. A dimorphic species, it has various plumage phases. White-throated form commonest. Some pied forms have black or yellowish smudges on breast.
• Small head crest sometimes evident.

Voice
• Croaks, clucks and coos at nest sites, otherwise silent.

◀ **Smudgy plumage phase of Little Shag.**
▼ **Little Shags.**

Food
• Dives from surface for fish, especially eels, crustaceans and insects.
• Does not fish in packs as does Little Black Shag.

Breeding
• *Time:* August to March.
• *Nest:* In small colonies in trees and low bushes, usually near water. Nest built of sticks and grasses.
• *Eggs:* Clutch of 3 or 4 pale-blue eggs with chalky covering. Both sexes incubate.

Distribution & Habitat
• Coastal waters throughout New Zealand. Also common on inland lakes and wetlands.
• Often fishes on small farm ponds and ditches.

5 White-faced Heron
Ardea novaehollandiae novaehollandiae

Family ARDEIDAE
Genus *Ardea*

Category
- Native. Self-introduced from Australia, rare till 1940s.

Field Characteristics
- 66 cm. Slimmer than marine Reef Heron.
- Prominent white face, light blue-grey body, and dark trailing edge to wings in flight. Immature coloration: generally similar to adult, but with indistinct white face.
- Slow, leisurely wingbeat. Neck folded in flight.
- Often occur in large flocks during winter, especially on mudflats.
- Often perches on trees and fence posts.

Voice
- Guttural croaks.

Food
- Wide range of small fish,

crustaceans, frogs, tadpoles, earthworms and insects (dragonflies, grasshoppers, blowflies, etc).
- Has habit of raking with foot to disturb invertebrates in tidal pools.

Breeding
- *Time:* As early as June or July in northern districts.
- *Nest:* of sticks, often flimsy, favourite site is in pine trees, macrocarpa or large pohutukawa trees.
- *Eggs:* 2 to 4 pale turquoise-coloured eggs. Both sexes incubate for 24 to 26 days.
- *Chicks:* fledge at 6 weeks.

Distribution & Habitat
- Most common heron, now widespread throughout New Zealand on sheltered seacoasts, estuaries, harbours, inland lakes and open farmland.

◀ **White-faced Heron.**
◀ **White-faced Heron in flight.**

6 Cattle Egret
Bubulcus ibis coromandus

Family ARDEIDAE
Genus *Bubulcus*

Category
- Native. Recently self-introduced from Australia. First reported in 1963 in Otago. Expanding distribution around world in temperate and tropical zones.

Field Characteristics
- 51 cm.
- Noticeable stocky build, stout yellow bill.
- White, with a buff crown and neck in late spring.
- Has a rapid wingbeat when compared with other herons.
- A wary bird. Usually seen in flocks, feeding around cattle for the disturbed insects and earth-worms. Sometimes observed in tidal estuaries.

Voice
- Silent.

Food
- Insects, grubs and earthworms.

Breeding
- Our birds return to New South Wales to nest in November. Not yet recorded as nesting in New Zealand.

Distribution & Habitat
- A late-autumn and winter migrant to New Zealand from Australia, flocks tend to revisit former locations. Numbers fluctuate from year to year.
- Inhabit pastureland, sometimes tidal estuaries.

◄ **Cattle Egrets.**
▼ **Cattle Egrets.**

Australasian Bittern/Matuku
Botaurus poiciloptilus

Family ARDEIDAE
Genus *Botaurus*

Category
• Native. Also found Australia and New Caledonia.

Field Characteristics
• 71 cm. Bulkier than White-faced Heron with shorter legs, and neck appearing stout and shorter.
• All buff-brown with dark streaking. Well camouflaged in raupo.
• Flight slow, with neck folded as with herons.
• Usually seen singly. When disturbed, either crouches low or points bill upward and freezes.
• Very secretive.

Voice
• Low guttural croaks.
• Male utters low booming call in breeding season from late August to early summer. More frequently heard in evening.
• Female utters watery bubbling call when approaching nest.

◀ **Australasian Bittern fishing in swamp.**
◀ **Australasian Bittern at nest.**

Food
• Freshwater fish, especially eels, frogs, tadpoles and insects.
• Reported to occasionally take small birds and mice.

Breeding
• *Time:* September to January.
• *Nest:* Female alone builds bulky nest of raupo and rushes in dense vegetation.
• *Eggs:* 3 to 6 olive-brown eggs laid at 2-day intervals. Incubation starts with laying of second egg. Female alone incubates for 24 to 26 days.
• *Chicks:* are fed by regurgitation; they leave nest and wander in surrounding vegetation when about 10 days old, and can fly when 5 weeks old.

Distribution & Habitat
• Throughout New Zealand in wetlands, swamps, especially when overgrown with reeds and raupo. Occasionally seen among mangroves.
• Numbers are decreasing due to loss of swamp habitat caused by draining for agricultural use.

Black Swan
Cygnus atratus

Family ANATIDAE
Genus *Cygnus*

Category
- Introduced as a game bird from Australia during 1860s in both North and South Islands.

Field Characteristics
- 130 cm.
- Black body. In flight, white wing-tips are conspicuous. Bill ruby red with white tip. Immature coloration: grey, with dark bill.
- Outstretched neck in flight, leisurely wingbeat.

Voice
- Trumpet, hiss and whistle.

Food
- Shoots of water plants and some invertebrates. Also goes ashore to graze pastures.

Breeding
- *Time:* Nest as early as June in the north, and through to December.
- *Nest:* Built of reeds and vegetation in stands of raupo and lakeside vegetation.
- *Eggs:* Clutch of 4 to 10, incubated by both sexes for 35 days.

Distribution & Habitat
- Very numerous on Lake Ellesmere, Rotorua lakes, Vernon Lagoons and several urban-park lakes.
- Also found in some marine habitats such as northern Kaipara Harbour.

▼ **Black Swans and cygnets.**

Canada Goose
Branta canadensis maxima

Family ANATIDAE
Genus *Branta*

Category
- Introduced to New Zealand in 1905 from North America. Recently introduced to North Island.

Field Characteristics
- 100 cm. Smaller than Black Swan, with shorter neck.
- Colour buff, with black neck and white cheeks. Immature coloration: black parts are dark brown.
- Outstretched neck in flight, fast wingbeat. Fly in a 'V' formation.

Voice
- Hoarse honking and trumpeting.

Food
- Graze vegetation and eat seeds. Graze farm pastures and cause fouling.

Breeding
- *Time:* Late September to November.
- *Nest:* Main nesting area is near headwaters of South Island rivers east of the Southern Alps. Nest of grasses lined with down built in vegetation.
- *Eggs:* 2 to 10 white eggs. Female alone incubates these for 30 days. Male usually on guard nearby.

Distribution & Habitat
- South Island high-country lakes and Lake Ellesmere. Becoming increasingly common on lakes in the North Island.
- Often seen on high country pastures in South Island.

▼ **Canada Geese.**

▲ Paradise Shelduck, female.

▲ Paradise Shelduck, male.

Paradise Shelduck/Putangitangi
Tadorna variegata

Family ANATIDAE
Genus *Tadorna*

Category
• Endemic.

Field Characteristics
• 63 cm. Size between Mallard and Canada Goose.
• Male has overall dark plumage, with metallic sheen on head. Female has dark back and rusty undersides, and conspicuous white head. Immature coloration: striped brown and white then similar to adult male.
• In flight, both sexes display white patches on wings.
• Usually seen in pairs in open country, also in flocks on lakes.

Voice
• A vocal bird when in flocks.
• A high-pitched honk is made by the male when disturbed.

◀ **Paradise Shelducks female and male with chicks.**

Food
• Graze pastures, eat lake weeds, seedheads of grasses, also insects and earthworms.

Breeding
• Birds pair for life.
• *Time:* Eggs laid August to October.
• *Nest:* In rock crevices, hollow logs, rabbit burrows, or under exposed tree roots. The nest of grasses is lined with down feathers.
• *Eggs:* Clutch of 6 to 12 white eggs. Incubation, only by female, for 31 days. Male assists in rearing young.

Distribution & Habitat
• Widely distributed throughout New Zealand.
• Open country and inland lakes and ponds. Also found in high altitude streams.

▲ Mallard, female, showing purple speculum.
▼ Mallard pair.

Mallard
Anas platyrhynchos platyrhynchos

Family ANATIDAE
Genus *Anas*

Category
- Introduced for game purposes from Europe and America since 1867. Liberations from hand-reared stock until 1950s.
- Comprises 80 per cent of New Zealand's dabbling ducks.

Field Characteristics
- 58 cm.
- The male has two plumages: the 'breeding plumage' as in the photo, and an 'eclipse' plumage (late summer and autumn) of drab brown. Male has olive-green bill. The female is somewhat similar to the Grey Duck, but is browner and distinguished by a blue or purple speculum (distinctive coloured area on wing) and orange-coloured legs. Dark olive-green bill. Immature coloration: similar to female.

▼ **Mallard in flight.**

- Dabbling or 'up-ending' is typical.

Voice
- Females quack. Males utter subdued 'guab-guab-guab'.

Food
- Vegetable matter, seeds, insects, grubs and earthworms.

Breeding
- *Time:* Eggs laid August to January.
- *Nest:* In poolside vegetation, or often some distance from the water. Built with grasses and lined with down.
- *Eggs:* 8 to 12 buff eggs, incubated by female for 28 days.

Distribution & Habitat
- Inhabits shallow-water ponds and lakes, also saltwater estuaries, lagoons and mudflats throughout New Zealand.

▲ Grey Duck, female, showing green speculum.

Grey Duck/Parera
Anas superciliosa superciliosa

Family ANATIDAE
Genus *Anas*

Category
- Native. Also Australia.
- In recent years numbers have been reduced by competition with introduced Mallard.

Field Characteristics
- 55 cm. Slightly smaller than Mallard.
- Duck and drake have similar brownish plumage, black stripe from bill through eye, otherwise face and chin light buff. Differ from female Mallard by white underwing and green speculum. Yellowish brown feet. Dark greyish blue bill.
- In shallow water, dabbling or 'up-ending' is typical.

Voice
- Female a quack, male utters soft 'guab-guab'.

◀ **Grey Duck and ducklings.**
▼ **Grey Duck, pair.**

Food
- Vegetable matter and seeds. Insects, snails and earthworms.

Breeding
- *Time:* in northern regions, nests as early as June, but usually August to December.
- *Nest:* Made of grasses lined with down, usually sited in rank vegetation but some nests are built several metres above ground in hollows or forks of trees.
- *Eggs:* Clutch of 6 to 10 cream-coloured eggs is incubated by female for 27 or 28 days.

Distribution & Habitat
- Throughout New Zealand, but more plentiful in north.
- Inhabits shallow freshwater rivers, streams, lagoons and alpine tarns. Occasionally seen in tidal estuaries.

▲ Grey Teal with duckling.

Grey Teal/Tete
Anas gracilis

Family ANATIDAE
Genus *Anas*

Category
- Native. Also Australia. A mobile species, many arriving from Australia.

Field Characteristics
- 43 cm. Much smaller than Grey Duck but often confused with it.
- Sexes alike. Show conspicuous white triangle on upper wing when in flight. Speculum is bluish-green.
- Rapid wingbeat, often seen in wheeling flocks.
- Dabbling (upending) when feeding.

Voice
- Female utters repeated rapid quack, male a hoarse rasping.

Food
- Shoots of water plants, insects and earthworms.

Breeding
- *Time:* Eggs laid June to January.
- *Nest:* of grasses is built in tree hollows, rabbit burrows or niggerheads. Grey Teal readily accept artificial nest-boxes.
- *Eggs:* Clutch of 6 to 8, cream-coloured, incubated by female for 24 to 26 days.

Distribution & Habitat
- Throughout both main islands, more plentiful since 1950s.
- Inhabits shallow lagoons and freshwater lakes which provide good shore cover.

◀ **Grey Teal feeding.**
▼ **Pair of Grey Teal.**

▲ New Zealand Shoveler, camouflaged.
▼ New Zealand Shoveler, female.

New Zealand Shoveler/Kuruwhengi
Anas rhynchotis variegata

Family ANATIDAE
Genus *Anas*

Category
- Endemic. Closely related race in Australia.

Field Characteristics
- 48 cm. Smaller than Mallard.
- Male's 'breeding plumage' has striking white facial crescent, prominent white patch on flank. 'Eclipse plumage' is similar to female. Female is similar to female Mallard but with powder-blue patch on upper wing.
- Conspicuous by its wide wedge-shaped bill which has lamellae (sieve-like appendages) along edges for filtering food from ooze.
- Our fastest flying duck. Conspicuous white wing-bar in flight. Feeds by dabbling.

Voice
- Usually fairly silent. Female gives a soft quack.

Food
- Seeds, insects and earthworms.

Breeding
- *Time:* Eggs laid August to December.
- *Nest:* of grasses lined with down. in thick vegetation near water.
- *Eggs:* Clutch of 6 to 10 cream-coloured eggs with blue tinge. Incubation by female for 26 days. Male assists in rearing young.

Distribution & Habitat
- Throughout New Zealand, but uncommon in Stewart Island.
- Inhabits lowland swamps and shallow lake edges. Often found in tidal harbours and off the coast during shooting season.

▼ **New Zealand Shoveler, male.**

▲ Group of New Zealand Scaup. ▼ New Zealand Scaup, male.

New Zealand Scaup/Papango
Aythya novaeseelandiae

Family ANATIDAE
Genus *Aythya*

Category
• Endemic.

Field Characteristics
• 40 cm. Plump and small.
• Dark plumage both sexes. Male has striking yellow eye and dark head. Female has white face patch in breeding plumage, dark eye. Conspicuous white wing-bar visible in flight.
• Usually seen in small flocks sitting on water.
• New Zealand's only true diving duck. Dives and swims submerged for 20 seconds or more.

Voice
• Females utter a subdued quack, males a low whistle.

▼ **New Zealand Scaup, female with ducklings.**

Food
• Dives for small fish and eats invertebrates and surface insects.

Breeding
• *Time:* Eggs laid from October to January.
• *Nest:* Composed of grasses and lined with down. Built in thick vegetation close to water.
• *Eggs:* Clutch of 5 to 8 cream-coloured eggs. Incubation by female for 28 days.

Distribution & Habitat
• Localised throughout both main islands.
• Inhabits clear-water lakes and lagoons, including mountain lakes. Not usually seen on shallow wetlands.

Australasian Harrier/Kahu
Circus approximans

Family ACCIPITRIDAE
Genus *Circus*

Category
- Native. Also found in Australia and Southwest Pacific.

Field Characteristics
- 60 cm. Large bird of prey.
- Brown plumage with light buff undersides, with dark streaking. Some old males appear almost white, with silvery grey wings. Immature coloration: chocolate brown.
- Leisurely flight compared with Falcon. Often soars with wings tipped upwards in a 'V' shape. Quarters the ground with slow wingbeat and glides in search of prey.
- Perches on posts.

Voice
- Usually silent. During nesting season utters high-pitched 'kee-kee'.

Food
- Large insects, lizards, frogs, birds and rodents. Occasionally catches fish and tadpoles.
- Frequently feeds on carrion, especially possums killed on road.

Breeding
- *Time:* In northern areas may nest as early as August, but usually October to November.
- *Nest:* Bulky, made of sticks, grasses and rushes, built in raupo swamps, clumps of pampas and occasionally in crown of tree fern.
- *Eggs:* 3 or 4 buff-coloured eggs. Incubation by female takes 29 to 32 days.
- *Chicks:* Incubation starts after laying of first egg so chicks are disproportionate in size and youngest chick seldom survives. Chicks fly when 6 weeks old.

Distribution & Habitat
- Widely distributed in open country throughout New Zealand and hunts along borders of forests.
- Non-breeding birds roost at night in communal roosts in sedge and raupo.

◀ **Australasian Harrier.**
◀ **Australasian Harrier and nest.**

▲ New Zealand Falcon, head, showing tubercle in nostril and dark eye.

◀ New Zealand Falcon.
▼ New Zealand Falcon at nest.

17 New Zealand Falcon/Karearea
Falco novaeseelandiae

Family FALCONIDAE
Genus *Falco*

Category
• Endemic.

Field Characteristics
• 45 cm. About half the size of Australasian Harrier.
• Female is markedly larger than male.
• Adult plumage is black striped with buff above, cream with dark streaks below. Thighs rusty red. Immature coloration is dark blackish brown above and dark chocolate brown streaked with fawn below.
• Rapid flight and long tail distinguish it from the larger Australasian Harrier.
• A tubercle (projection) in the nostril opening distinguishes it from Australasian Harrier.

Voice
• Rapid, repeated 'kek-kek-kek', also a subdued high-pitched scream, especially in immature birds.

Food
• Main diet appears to be smaller passerine (perching) birds, especially starlings, skylarks and finches.
• Also large insects, lizards and rodents.

Breeding
• *Time:* September to December.
• *Nest:* No nesting material used. Eggs are laid in a depression on the ground under overhanging rocks, fallen logs or on ledges of rocky bluffs. Bush Falcons also reported to occasionally nest in clumps of perching epiphytes.
• *Eggs:* Clutch of 3 eggs are buff, heavily blotched with dark russet-brown markings. Incubation is by both sexes for 30 to 33 days.
• *Chicks:* Fed by female with food captured by the male. The smaller male chicks fly when 32 days old and female chicks when 35 days old.

Distribution & Habitat
• Eastern race inhabits South Island high country, the southern race Fiordland. The Bush Falcon inhabits forested and open country regions of Westland and the North Island.
• Rarely found north of the central North Island.

California Quail
Callipepla californica brunnescens

Family PHASIANIDAE
Genus *Callipepla*

Category
- Introduced from USA 1862.

Field Characteristics
- 25 cm.
- Prominent head crest in male, smaller crest in female. Male's white face is surrounded by white band.
- Runs rapidly and flies with rapid wingbeat. Rises with a rapid whirring when disturbed.
- Often perches on fenceposts.

Voice
- Calls 'Miss Harper' or 'tobacco'.

Food
- Seeds and fruits of many plants, also shoots, leaves and a few insects.

Breeding
- *Time:* Nests from September to February.
- *Nest:* Composed of grasses, hidden under log or in dense vegetation, often under fallen manuka or gorse.
- *Eggs:* Clutch of 10 to 18 cream-coloured eggs, blotched and streaked with light brown, is incubated by hen for 23 days.

Distribution & Habitat
- Found throughout the country, plentiful in some areas.
- Inhabits scrub and open land, occasionally in gardens.
- Often seen in coveys or family groups.

▼ **California Quail.**

19 Chukor
Alectoris chukar

Family PHASIANIDAE
Genus *Alectoris*

Category
• Introduced from Persia and Pakistan in the 1920s.

Field Characteristics
• 33 cm.
• Overall grey plumage with conspicuous black and white bars on flank. White cheeks and throat bordered by black band. Red legs and beak.
• Loud whirring of wings in flight.
• Usually seen in coveys or family groups.

Food
• Seeds, shoots, leaves and berries.

Voice
• A repeated 'chuck-chuck'.

Breeding
• *Time:* September to January.
• *Nest:* Built of grasses under rock or in thick vegetation.
• *Eggs:* Clutch of 10 to 20 cream-coloured eggs with purple blotches. Female incubates for 24 days.

Distribution & Habitat
• Inhabit high, dry, rocky country in the South Island east of the Alps.
• Localised in certain areas of the Bay of Plenty.

▼ Chukor.

Ring-necked Pheasant
Phasianus colchicus

Family PHASIANIDAE
Genus *Phasianus*

Category
- Introduced to New Zealand in the 1840s.
- Wild stock still supplemented by annual liberations.

Field Characteristics
- 60 to 80 cm. Female slightly smaller than male.
- Long barred tail and bright colours, unlike other game birds. Most males have white neck ring, though overall colours vary through hybridisation. Ring-necked Pheasants interbreed with the introduced Black-necked variety. Hen is of overall brown colour and has a shorter tail.

Voice
- Cock bird utters three-syllable 'croork', with rustle of wings.

Food
- Seeds, fruits, green shoots and leaves, and insects.

Breeding
- Polygamous. Male accompanies 3 or 4 females.
- *Time:* Eggs are laid from September to January.
- *Nest:* Made of grasses, scantily lined. Built in thick vegetation.
- *Eggs:* 6 to 14 olive-brown eggs, incubated by hen for 23 days. Only female cares for young.

Distribution & Habitat
- Common in the north of North Island. Apart from in the Nelson region, it is not common in the South Island.
- Inhabits scrub, open country and farmland.

▼ **Ring-necked Pheasant, male.**

Banded Rail/Moho-pereru
Rallus philippensis assimilis

Family RALLIDAE
Genus *Rallus*

Category
- Native. Also Southeast Asia, Australia, and Southwest Pacific.

Field Characteristics
- 30 cm.
- Black and white striped pattern on underside. Pronounced chestnut eye streak forming collar at the back of neck.
- Often seen running rapidly among mangroves. Although a strong flier, appears reluctant to take to the air when disturbed.
- Very secretive.

Voice
- High-pitched, penetrating squeak; low growling and grunting sounds near nest.

Food
- Crustaceans, insects and earthworms.

Breeding
- *Time:* In northern districts nesting starts in August; probably double-brooded, as nesting as late as February has been recorded.
- *Nests:* of sedges and grasses are built, well hidden in salt-marsh sedges or thick herbage, near or above water.
- *Eggs:* Clutch of 2 to 5 buff-coloured eggs with dark brown blotches is incubated for 18 or 19 days by both sexes.

Distribution & Habitat
- Found mainly north of Bay of Plenty, also Northwest Nelson and Stewart Island.
- Inhabits mangrove swamps, salt marshes and wetlands; also follows streams into farmlands.

Continued ▶

▼ **Banded Rail on nest.**

◀ Banded Rail approaching nest.
▼ Banded Rail.

Spotless Crake/Puweto
Porzana tabuensis plumbea

Family RALLIDAE
Genus *Porzana*

Category
• Native. Also found in Australia and Southwest Pacific.

Field Characteristics
• 20 cm.
• All dark plumage, appears dark grey.
• Prominent red eye.
• Swims and dives readily, rarely flies.
• Seldom seen in the open. Very secretive and crepuscular (active at dawn and dusk) in habit. Readily responds to tape-recorded calls.

Voice
• A rattling warble and repeated musical 'dook-dook'.

Food
• Insects, grubs, earthworms and tadpoles.

Breeding
• *Time:* August to November.
• *Nest:* Commonest site is in clump of small cutty grass within a raupo swamp. The nest, composed of grasses and reeds, is usually sited half to 1 metre above water level.
• *Eggs:* Clutch of 2 or 3 dark buff-coloured eggs with dark markings. Both sexes incubate for 19 to 22 days.

Distribution & Habitat
• Inhabits swamps throughout New Zealand.
• Even small pockets of raupo and swamp often harbour a few birds.

▼ **Spotless Crake at nest.**

▲ Pukeko at nest with newly hatched chick.

▼ Pukeko, showing large feet.

▼ Pukeko swimming.

Pukeko
Porphyrio porphyrio melanotus

Family RALLIDAE
Genus *Porphyrio*

Category
- Native. A cosmopolitan species, it is also found in Australia and South Africa.

Field Characteristics
- 51 cm.
- Both sexes bright blue and black. Red bill, frontal shield and legs. Often flicks tail to show white under tail coverts (the small feathers surrounding the base of larger feathers).
- Runs fast. Reluctant flier, and flies clumsily with dangling legs. In spite of this, can fly long distances. Swims well.
- In some areas birds live as communities, others have been seen in pairs.

Voice
- Raucous high-pitched screech; subdued, musical 'tuk-tuk'.

Food
- Mainly feeds on vegetable matter. Shoots are held in foot, parrot fashion.
- Also feeds on invertebrates and robs eggs from nests.

Breeding
- *Time:* Pukekos nest during many months of the year, but usually August to January.
- *Nest:* Single pairs nest in raupo swamps or in clumps of rushes in paddocks or rank grass. In communities, two or more females lay in one nest and incubation is shared by several birds. The nest is composed of grasses and rushes.
- *Eggs:* Single pairs lay from 3 to 6 buff-coloured eggs with dark spots and blotches; communal birds may incubate up to 12 eggs. Incubation period is 24 days.

Distribution & Habitat
- Common in wetter areas throughout New Zealand.
- Inhabits swamps, marshes, lake edges and pastures which have clumps of rushes.

▲ Australian Coot feeding chick. ▼ Australian Coot.

Australian Coot
Fulica atra australis

Family RALLIDAE
Genus *Fulica*

Category
- Native. Self-introduced from Australia since 1958.

Field Characteristics
- 38 cm. Slightly smaller than Pukeko.
- All black with contrasting white bill and frontal shield. Immature coloration: grey with dark bill.
- Most aquatic of the rail family, seldom comes ashore. Has jerking head when swimming. Dives frequently for food.
- Flies strongly. Often seen in flocks after nesting season.

Voice
- A penetrating, reed-like 'kraak'.

▼ **Pair of Australian Coots at nest.**

Food
- Mainly vegetable matter such as shoots from water plants, also invertebrates.

Breeding
- *Time:* Eggs laid from August to January.
- *Nest:* Constructed of reed stems and raupo, well hidden in cover of reed beds or on low willow branches trailing in water.
- *Eggs:* Clutch of 3 to 6 cream-coloured eggs with dark spots. Both sexes incubate for 21 to 23 days. Two or more broods are raised each season.

Distribution & Habitat
- Found throughout New Zealand in freshwater lakes which have a fringe of raupo or reeds.

Spur-winged Plover
Vanellus miles novaehollandiae

Family CHARADRIIDAE
Genus *Vanellus*

Category
- Native. Self-introduced to Southland from Australia in 1930s.

Field Characteristics
- 38 cm. The size of a Rock Pigeon.
- Both sexes the same. Recognised by black head with prominent yellow wattles. Crown and shoulders black, back brown, white below.
- Long legs and lapwing flight with slow wingbeat.
- Seen in flocks in autumn.

Voice
- A loud rattling call.

◄ **Spur-winged Plovers and nest.**
◄ **Spur-winged Plover chick.**
▼ **A flock of Spur-winged Plovers.**

Food
- Insects, grubs and earthworms, also marine crustaceans.

Breeding
- *Time:* Nest as early as June in northern regions, with later broods in November and December.
- *Nest:* A depression in ground lined with few grasses, in paddocks or stony ground.
- *Eggs:* Lay 2 to 4 dark-brown heavily blotched eggs. Incubation shared by sexes for 30 days.

Distribution & Habitat
- Throughout New Zealand.
- Inhabits open-country pastures, riverbeds, shorelines of lakes and sheltered coasts.

26 Barbary Dove
Streptopelia roseogrisea

Family COLUMBIDAE
Genus *Streptopelia*

Category
- Introduced from North Africa in 1970s.

Field Characteristics
- 28 cm.
- Pale buff colour with prominent black ring on neck.
- Often feeds on ground beneath trees.

Voice
- A repeated soft 'coo-cruu'.

Food
- Seeds, fruits and occasional insects.

Breeding
- Time: August to March.
- *Nest:* Flimsy, made of twigs in fork of tree or shrub.
- *Eggs:* 2 white eggs. Incubated by both sexes.

Distribution & Habitat
- Auckland, Bay of Plenty, Hawke's Bay and Wairarapa.
- Inhabits open country with trees, and urban parks.

▼ **Barbary Doves.**

Spotted Dove
Streptopelia chinensis tigrina

Family COLUMBIDAE
Genus *Streptopelia*

Category
• Recently introduced from Asia.

Field Characteristics
• 30 cm.
• Overall rosy-fawn colour.
• Strong, low direct flight.

Voice
• A repeated 'coo-cruu'.

Food
• Seeds, fruits and insects.
• Large flocks regularly feed on seeds from dried sludge at sewage works.

Breeding
• *Time:* August to March.
• *Nest:* Flimsy, made of fine twigs built in tree fork or shrub.
• *Eggs:* 2 white eggs. Incubated by both sexes.

Distribution & Habitat
• Common around Auckland and spreading to Northern Waikato.
• Inhabits open farmland with trees, and urban parks.

▼ Spotted Doves.

Rock Pigeon
Columba livia

Family COLUMBIDAE
Genus *Columba*

Category
- Introduced from Europe in 1860s as domesticated races and now wild.

Field Characteristics
- 33 cm.
- Colour forms vary from dark grey to light brown or even almost white. Sexes similar.

Voice
- Usually only males vocal, uttering a repeated 'coodly-coo'.

Food
- Wide variety of seeds, grain from farmlands, legumes, fallen fruits and occasionally insects.

Breeding
- *Time:* Rock Pigeons nest throughout the year.
- *Nest:* on ledges of rocky cliffs or buildings. Sparse nest material of grasses and small twigs.
- *Eggs:* Lay two white eggs. Both sexes incubate for 18 days.

Distribution & Habitat
- Throughout New Zealand.
- Many birds inhabit city parks, others are found in open country with cliffs and rocky terrain for roosting and nesting. Usually seen in small flocks feeding on riverbeds, farmlands or seashore.

▼ **Rock Pigeon.**

Sulphur-crested Cockatoo
Cacatua galerita

Family CACATUIDAE
Genus *Cacatua*

Category
- Introduced as cage escapees or self-introduced from Australia.

Field Characteristics
- 50 cm.
- White, with sulphur crest.
- Usually seen in flocks feeding on ground, also in trees.
- Very wary and difficult to approach closely.

Voice
- A raucous screech.

Food
- Seeds, fruits, buds and leaves, also insects.

Breeding
- *Time:* October to January.
- *Nest:* In tree cavity, usually built high up. Also nests reported in baled haystacks.
- *Eggs:* In Australia, reported to lay 3 or 4 white eggs, incubated for 30 days.

Distribution & Habitat
- Established from Waikato Heads to Raglan, also near Wanganui and in parts of Northern Wairarapa, Manawatu and Wellington Province. Recent reports locate some in Kaipara area and on Northland's west coast.
- Inhabit open country with small pockets of forest for roosting.

▼ **Sulphur-crested Cockatoo.**

Little Owl
Athene noctua

Family STRIGIDAE
Genus *Athene*

Category
- Introduced from Europe to Otago, 1906.

Field Characteristics
- 23 cm. Smaller, squatter and lighter in colour than Morepork.
- Rounded head and wings.
- Has a low, bouncing flight. Often seen perched on posts or power poles during daylight.

Voice
- A high-pitched 'tiew' call. Also mewing sounds during nesting.

◄ **Little Owl at nest hole.**
◄ **Little Owl, pair.**
▼ **Little Owl chick.**

Food
- Mainly insects and earthworms, also small birds occasionally.

Breeding
- *Time:* September to December.
- *Nests:* in holes in trees, rabbit burrows and stacks of hay bales. Negligible nest material.
- *Eggs:* 2 to 4 round, white eggs incubated by female for 28 days.

Distribution & Habitat
- South Island.
- Inhabits open country and farmland, also small pine plantations. Does not penetrate forests.

▲ New Zealand Kingfisher, male.
▼ Male Kingfisher feeding newly fledged chick.

New Zealand Kingfisher/Kotare
Halcyon sancta vagans

Family ALCEDINIDAE
Genus *Halcyon*

Category
• Native. Also Australia.

Field Characteristics
• 24 cm.
• Bright greenish blue above and off-white to buff below. Male more brightly coloured than female. Russet on flanks and underwing fades in summer. Immature coloration: duller, with darker mottled breast.
• Large black pointed bill. Very short legs.
• A wary bird. Often seen perched on rocks, posts, powerlines and trees as vantage points, waiting to capture prey.
• Direct flight.

Voice
• Repeated 'kek-kek-kek'.
• During courtship a vibrating 'keree-keree' with rising inflection.
• Short 'krek' when boring holes.

Food
• Insects and their larvae, earthworms, spiders, tadpoles, fish, crabs, freshwater crayfish, skinks, small birds and mice.

Breeding
• *Time:* Eggs laid November to January.
• *Nest:* Bores tunnels in clay banks or rotting tree trunks, or uses cavities in trees.
• *Eggs:* 4 or 5 white eggs. Incubation shared by sexes, but mainly by female.
• *Chicks:* Both parents feed chicks, which fledge when 26 days old. Fed by parents for further 10 days.

Distribution & Habitat
• Common throughout New Zealand, especially in coastal regions of the northern North Island.
• Lives in marine habitats, wet lands, open country, along water courses, farmland and forests. Migrates to coastal areas during winter months.

Skylark
Alauda arvensis

Family ALAUDIDAE
Genus *Alauda*

Category
- Introduced from Europe in 1860s.

Field Characteristics
- 18 cm. Plumper build and less confiding than Pipit.
- Brown above, buff below.
- Has head crest, which is raised when startled.
- Rapid wingbeat while ascending in a spiral to great heights when singing and then slowly descending.

Voice
- Sings a continuous trilling song while soaring upwards.

Food
- Insects, their larvae, spiders and seeds.

Breeding
- *Time:* Eggs laid September to January.
- *Nest:* Composed of a few fine grasses, built in depression in ground, usually in short pasture.
- *Eggs:* 3 to 5 greyish, heavily speckled eggs. Incubation, only by female, for 11 days.
- *Chicks:* Fed by both parents.

Distribution & Habitat
- Common throughout New Zealand.
- Inhabit open country, farmland, sand dunes and sub-alpine herb fields.

▼ **Skylark in sand dune habitat.**

New Zealand Pipit/Pihoihoi

Anthus novaeseelandiae novaeseelandiae

Family MOTACILLIDAE
Genus *Anthus*

Category
- Native. Very similar species throughout world.

Field Characteristics
- 19 cm. Slimmer than Skylark.
- Colouring similar to Skylark, but greyer.
- No crest. Light eye stripe more prominent.
- Persistent tail flicking. Does not soar high.

Voice
- Slightly rasping 'zuit' or 'cheet'.

Food
- Insects and their larvae, sand hoppers, kelp flies, also seeds.

Breeding
- *Time:* September to February.
- *Nest:* of grasses, built in rough grass and herbage, often under a plant, usually on side of bank.
- *Eggs:* Clutch of 3 or 4 cream-coloured eggs with dark blotches. Double brooded. Incubation by female for 15 days.
- *Chicks:* Fed by both parents.

Distribution & Habitat
- Throughout New Zealand.
- Inhabits rough grasslands, sand dunes and rocky terrain. Often lives at high altitudes.

▼ **New Zealand Pipit at nest.**

▲ Welcome Swallow.

34 Welcome Swallow
Hirundo tahitica neoxena

Family HIRUNDINIDAE
Genus *Hirundo*

Category
- Native. Self-introduced to Northland from Australia in 1950s. Rare stragglers prior to 1950s.
- Also Southwest Pacific and Australia.

Field Characteristics
- 15 cm. Smaller than House Sparrow.
- Glossy bluish-black with chestnut face and throat.
- Strongly forked tail.
- Swift circling flight, sometimes splashing on surface of water. Often seen in groups perched on fences or telephone lines.

Voice
- A high-pitched 'zwitt', also a chatter.

◀ **Welcome Swallow flying to nest.**
▼ **Welcome Swallows.**

Food
- Insects caught on wing. In winter often feeds on kelp flies on beaches.

Breeding
- *Time:* Three or more broods a year from August to February.
- *Nest:* Built of mud and grasses lined with feathers, attached to wall of culvert, bridge or ledges of buildings.
- *Eggs:* Clutch of 3 to 5 pale-pink eggs spotted with brown. Incubation by female for 15 days.
- *Chicks:* Both parents feed chicks, which fledge when 18 days old.

Distribution & Habitat
- Common throughout New Zealand.
- Lives near lakes, rivers, swamps and seashore.

▲ Female Blackbird at nest.　▼ Male Blackbird sunning.

35 Blackbird
Turdus merula

Family MUSCICAPIDAE
Genus *Turdus*

Category
- Introduced from Europe in 1860s.

Field Characteristics
- 25 cm.
- Male glossy black with orange bill. Female has uniform dark brown above, lighter below, with inconspicuous streaks on throat, lightly spotted breast, grey chin, bill generally brown. Immature: dark brown with buff streaking on back and rusty brown undersides with dark streaks and speckles.

Voice
- Melodious flute-like whistle. Alarm note is a cackle.

Food
- Insects, grubs and earthworms. Wide variety of fruits, including native podocarps, shrubs and nikau palm.
- Cause damage in orchards.

Breeding
- *Time:* 3 or more broods a year, eggs laid from July to January.
- *Nest:* Bulky, made of twigs, leaves and grasses fortified with mud, in trees, shrubs, hedges, and frequently on or in buildings.
- *Eggs:* 3 to 5 greenish-coloured eggs blotched with light brown. Female incubates for 13 days.
- *Chicks:* Both parents feed chicks. Fledge 14 days.

Distribution & Habitat
- Common throughout New Zealand.
- Inhabit gardens, parks, orchards and farmlands. Also found in depths of native forest, where it is extremely wary.

▼ **Male Blackbird.**

Song Thrush
Turdus philomelos

Family MUSCICAPIDAE
Genus *Turdus*

Category
- Introduced from Europe 1860s.

Field Characteristics
- 23 cm.
- Sexes similar. Uniform olive brown above, undersides light buff with bold dark brown spots on breast and flank. White belly.
- When feeding, hops and runs, then remains motionless.

Voice
- Harsher than blackbird song. Passages repeated three times and followed by pause and descending notes.

Food
- Insects, grubs and earthworms, also snails broken open on favourite rock. Also takes some fruits.

Breeding
- *Time:* Several broods from June to January.
- *Nest:* of twigs and grasses with lining of mud built in shrubs, generally low and inconspicuous.
- *Eggs:* 3 to 5 blue eggs with black spots. Incubation by female for 12 days.
- *Chicks:* Both parents feed chicks, which fledge at 14 days.

Distribution & Habitat
- Common throughout New Zealand.
- Found in gardens, parks, orchards and farmlands. Also high country above 1500 metres. Rarely seen in depths of forest.

▼ Song Thrush at nest.

Hedge Sparrow (Dunnock)
Prunella modularis

Family PRUNELLIDAE
Genus *Prunella*

Category
- Introduced, originally from Europe in 1860s.
- Not protected.

Field Characteristics
- 14 cm. Similar in size to House Sparrow, but slimmer.
- Sexes similar. Blue-grey on breast, streaked brown on back.
- Moves in short hops with body inclined forward, flicking movements of wings and raised tail.
- Short straight flight.
- Secretive, usually staying close to cover. Often heard singing in gardens, yet unseen. Never high above ground except male on song perch.

Voice
- A melodious, high-pitched warbled whistle.

Food
- Insects, spiders, grubs and small earthworms, also a few seeds.

Breeding
- *Time:* Eggs laid from September to January. Double brooded.
- *Nest:* Very neat, composed of fine grasses and moss, built in thick shrub.
- *Eggs:* 3 or 4 bright turquoise-coloured eggs. Incubation by hen for 11 days.
- *Chicks:* Fed by both parents. Fledge at 12 days.

Distribution & Habitat
- Common throughout New Zealand.
- Inhabits open country with shrubs and scrub. Seen in fell-fields at over 1000 metres and in suburban gardens.

▼ **Hedge Sparrow.**

38 North Island Fernbird/Matata
Bowdleria punctata vealeae

South Island Fernbird/Matata
Bowdleria punctata punctata

Family SYLVIIDAE
Genus *Bowdleria*

Category
• Endemic. Six subspecies.

Field Characteristics
• 18 cm. Sparrow sized.
• Uniform olive brown above, undersides light buff with bold dark brown spots on breast and flank. White splash above eye. The South Island Fernbird has larger dark spots on breast. The Stewart Island Fernbird *B.p. stewartiana* has more golden plumage.
• Longish tail with disjointed barbs.
• A very weak flier and rarely seen unless flushed. Responds well to tape-recorded calls.
• Makes mouse-like progression through undergrowth.

Voice
• At least five different calls. Common 'u-tick' uttered by two birds as contact.
• Male calls 'too-lit' with rising second note, also single 'trup'.

◄ **North Island Fernbird.**

Food
• Entirely insects, grubs and nursery-web spiders.

Breeding
• *Time:* Eggs laid from September to January.
• *Nest:* Loose cup of dried grasses, lined with few feathers, built in sedges or raupo, usually 15 cm above ground or water, but sometimes over 1 metre in matted *Plagianthus.*
• *Eggs:* Clutch of 2 to 4 pinkish-coloured eggs with brown spots. Both sexes incubate for 14 or 15 days.

Distribution & Habitat
• North Island Fernbird is common in swamps of Northland and central Volcanic Plateau, also in flax and scrub, uncommon in southern regions.
• South Island subspecies has a restricted range and is uncommon in Canterbury.

▲ Male Yellowhammer drinking.

Yellowhammer
Emberiza citrinella

Family EMBERIZIDAE
Genus *Emberiza*

Category
• Introduced from Europe 1860s.

Field Characteristics
• 16 cm. Larger than House Sparrow.
• Male has bright yellow head and undersides with dark chest band; yellower than female.
• Both sexes have conspicuous russet rump, and mainly white outer tail feathers, prominent in flight.
• Congregate in large flocks in winter to feed on paddocks.

Voice
• Contact note is a metallic 'tink'.
• Males have song of 9 or 10 notes.

◄ **Male Yellowhammer.**

Food
• Mainly seeds from grasses and many other plants.
• Also takes insects, grubs and spiders.

Breeding
• *Time:* October to January.
• *Nest:* Made of dry grasses and moss, lined with finer grasses and hair. Built low down in thick herbage, especially in brambles.
• *Eggs:* Clutch of 3 or 4 pinkish eggs with 'pencil mark' lines and dark spots. Incubation by female for 13 days.

Distribution & Habitat
• Throughout New Zealand.
• Very common in open country, scrub and sand dunes.

◄ **Female Yellowhammer.**

▲ Chaffinch, female.

Chaffinch
Fringilla coelebs

Family FRINGILLIDAE
Genus *Fringilla*

Category
- Introduced from Europe 1860s.

Field Characteristics
- 15 cm.
- Male has pinky red colouring and is brighter than light brown female. Both sexes have two conspicuous white bars on wing and white outer tail feathers prominent in flight.
- In forest, call note is usually heard before bird is seen.
- Often feeds on ground.

Voice
- Common call note is a metallic 'chink'.
- Male's song is a bright 'chip-chip-chip-pell-pell-cheery-cheery-cheeoo'.

Food
- Mainly seeds, which are crushed, not opened as with other finches.
- Also fruits and insects.

Breeding
- *Time:* September to January.
- *Nest:* An extremely neat, well-camouflaged nest of grasses and lichens. In a tree fork or shrub.
- *Eggs:* Clutch of 3 to 5 greyish-coloured eggs with purple spots. Incubated by female for 12 days.

Distribution & Habitat
- Our commonest finch, widespread throughout New Zealand.
- Inhabits open country with trees, suburban parks and gardens, and is often found in the depths of native and exotic forests.

◀ Chaffinch, male.
▼ Chaffinch, male at nest.

▲ Greenfinch, pair at nest.

Greenfinch
Carduelis chloris

Family FRINGILLIDAE
Genus *Carduelis*

Category
- Introduced from Britain in 1860s. Now commoner here than in Britain.

Field Characteristics
- 15 cm. Larger than House Sparrow.
- Male olive green, with bright yellow markings on wings and tail very prominent in flight. Female and immature coloration is duller and browner.
- Heavy, pale bill. Forked tail.
- Form large flocks during autumn and winter.

Voice
- A buzzing 'zwee'.

Food
- Mainly seeds from grasses and other plants, also insects.

Breeding
- *Time:* September to January.
- *Nest:* Largish, made of twigs, grasses and moss. Built in fork of shrubs.
- *Eggs:* Clutch of 3 or 4 light-grey eggs with brown spots and blotches. Incubated by female for 11 or 12 days.

Distribution & Habitat
- Common throughout New Zealand.
- Inhabit open country, orchards and suburban gardens.

◄ Male Greenfinch at nest.
▼ Greenfinch, pair at nest.

Goldfinch
Carduelis carduelis

Family FRINGILLIDAE
Genus *Carduelis*

Category
- Introduced from Britain in 1860s. Now commoner here than in country of origin.

Field Characteristics
- 12.5 cm. Smaller than House Sparrow.
- Sexes similar in colour: distinctive red, white and black head. Broad yellow band on black wings. Immature: streaky light brown underside and lacks bright head colours.
- Small size and bright plumage distinguish it from other finches.
- Forms very large flocks of over 1000 birds in open country in winter.

Voice
- A high-pitched 'piew'.

▼ **Goldfinch.**

Food
- Variety of seeds from Scotch thistles and grasses.
- Also eats insects and their larvae.

Breeding
- *Time:* September to January. Usually two broods.
- *Nest:* Neat, made of grasses, moss and lichens, lined with thistledown. Often built in orchard trees or gorse.
- *Eggs:* Clutch of 3 to 6 light-grey eggs with dark spots is incubated by female for 11 days. Male feeds her on nest.

Distribution & Habitat
- Common throughout New Zealand.
- Inhabits orchards, open country with trees and suburban gardens.

43 Redpoll
Carduelis flammea

Family FRINGILLIDAE
Genus *Carduelis*

Category
- Introduced from Britain in 1860s.

Field Characteristics
- 12 cm. The smallest finch. Smaller than House Sparrow.
- Superficially drab, has crimson forehead and black bib. Pink breast of male (sometimes absent) is seen at close quarters. Immature: crimson on forehead is absent.
- Has undulating flight.
- Flocks after nesting.

Voice
- A constant twitter in flight.

Food
- Seeds and shoots.
- Buds of fruit trees in orchards.

Breeding
- *Time:* September to January. Often two broods.
- *Nest:* Compact, made of grasses and moss, lined with wool or hair. Built in low bushes, especially gorse.
- *Eggs:* Clutch of 3 to 5 greenish eggs with dark-brown spots is incubated by female for 11 days.

Distribution & Habitat
- Throughout New Zealand.
- Inhabit open country. Often seen at high altitudes, as well as in scrub and sand dunes.

▼ Redpoll.

PHOTO: D.W. HADDEN

House Sparrow
Passer domesticus

Family PLOCEIDAE
Genus *Passer*

Category
- Introduced from Europe in 1860s.

Field Characteristics
- 14 cm.
- Russet brown top with grey undersides. Males have a black bib varying in size. Also black bill in breeding season, otherwise brown. Females and immature birds are plainer, without bib or as much brown on top.
- Gregarious and usually seen in small flocks. Roost in flocks.

Voice
- Chirps and chatters.

◄ House Sparrow, male at left, with two females.
▼ House Sparrow, female, at nest.

Food
- Wide variety of seeds, green foliage of vegetables, fruits of native plants and trees, insects.
- Causes damage to cereal crops.

Breeding
- *Time:* July to April. Several broods.
- *Nest:* Bulky, untidy, domed nest composed of grasses and lined with feathers. Built in trees, cavities of cliffs and in buildings.
- *Eggs:* Clutch of 3 to 6 eggs of very variable colours, mainly grey and spotted, incubated by both sexes.

Distribution & Habitat
- Very common throughout New Zealand.
- Inhabit farmland, parks and suburban gardens.

▲ Newly fledged Starling chicks. ▼ Starling.

Starling
Sturnus vulgaris

Family STURNIDAE
Genus *Sturnus*

Category
• Introduced from Europe 1860s.

Field Characteristics
• 21 cm. Slightly smaller than Blackbird.
• After summer moult both sexes have spotted plumage. Tips of feathers later wear to produce spring glossy plumage. Immature coloration is dull brownish buff with dark bill.
• Often feed and roost in large flocks, outside of breeding season.

Voice
• Guttural warblings and chuckles.
• Imitate other birds' calls.

Food
• Wide range of insects, grubs, earthworms, snails, small fruits and nectar from flax flowers.
• Also takes fruit from native trees such as kahikatea.

Breeding
• *Time:* October to December.
• *Nest:* Often bulky, composed of grasses, small sticks, paper, leaves and feathers. Built in tree holes, crevices in cliffs and in buildings. Readily use garden nestboxes.
• *Eggs:* 3 to 5 pale-blue eggs. Both parents incubate for 11 days.
• *Chicks:* Fledge at 18 days.

Distribution & Habitat
• Common throughout New Zealand.
• Inhabit open country, farm pastures, parks, suburban gardens and seashores.

▼ Starling in autumn plumage.

▼ Starling in early summer plumage.

▲ Common Myna at nest hole.

Common Myna
Acridotheres tristis

Family STURNIDAE
Genus *Acridotheres*

Category
• Introduced from Australia in 1870s, originally from India.

Field Characteristics
• 24 cm. Similar size to Blackbird but shorter tail.
• Brown with blacker head. Bright yellow bill, legs and bare patch below eye. Conspicuous white patch on wing and tip of tail in flight. Immature bird has grey-brown head.
• Seen in small groups after nesting season. Use communal roosts in thick shrubs or bamboo.

Voice
• Raucous squawking, chattering and gurgling.

Food
• Insects, grubs, earthworms, fruits and carrion.
• Also predate nests of small birds and evict starlings from nests.

Breeding
• *Time:* Late nesters: November to January.
• *Nest:* Bulky, composed of small sticks, grasses, leaves, paper, plastic and feathers. Built in hole in tree, rock crevice, building or disused kingfisher burrows.
• *Eggs:* Lay 2 or 3 pale-blue eggs. Incubation, mainly by female, for 14 days.

Distribution & Habitat
• Seen throughout North Island, especially common in Northland. Absent from South Island.
• Inhabits open country, suburban areas and rubbish tips.

◀ **Common Myna.**
▼ **Common Myna flying to nest.**

Australian Magpie
Gymnorhina tibicen

Family CRACTICIDAE
Genus *Gymnorhina*

Category
- Introduced from Australia in 1860s.

Field Characteristics
- 42 cm.
- Two subspecies: White-backed Magpie *G.t. hypoleuca* and Black-backed Magpie *G. t. tibicen.* Frequently interbreed. Females and immature birds have grey-flecked backs.

Voice
- A melodious warble of flute-like notes.

Food
- Omnivorous. Wide variety of invertebrates, seeds, vegetation and carrion.
- Also lizards and eggs and young from ground-nesting birds.

Breeding
- *Time:* In the north often nests as early as June. Generally, August to November.
- *Nest:* Made of sticks lined with grasses and wool. Built in fork of tree, especially pines and macrocarpa. Defends nesting territory by dive-bombing intruders.
- *Eggs:* Clutch of 2 to 4 grey-blue eggs with dark blotches is incubated by female for 20 days.
- *Chicks:* Fed by both sexes.

Distribution & Habitat
- Widespread throughout New Zealand.
- Inhabits open country, especially farm pastures with trees.

▼ **White-backed Magpie, female.**

▼ **White-backed Magpie, male at nest.**

Rook
Corvus frugilegus

Family CORVIDAE
Genus *Corvus*

Category
- Introduced from Europe 1870s.

Field Characteristics
- 45 cm. Bigger than Australian Magpie.
- All black with bluish gloss and large bill.
- Only adults have bare grey skin surrounding base of bill.
- Has deliberate wing beat.
- A wary bird. Usually seen in groups feeding on farmland.
- Roosts at night in communal roosts.

Voice
- Repeated 'kaaw'.

Food
- A wide range of invertebrates, foliage of plants and walnuts.
- Frequently damage growing vegetable crops.

Breeding
- *Time:* September to December.
- *Nest:* Generally in colonies called rookeries, high up in pines, gums and oak trees. Built of sticks and lined with grasses and wool, sometimes reinforced with mud.
- *Eggs:* Clutch of 3 to 6 greenish-coloured eggs with dark brown blotches. Incubated by female for 17 or 18 days. Fed on nest by male.
- *Chicks:* Fledge when 33 days old.

Distribution & Habitat
- Widely distributed from Northern Hawke's Bay to Wairarapa, with smaller populations in Canterbury and Miranda, Firth of Thames.
- Chiefly inhabit farmlands.

▼ **Rook at nest.**

Index of Common Names

Index of Scientific Names